HOW TO STOP DATING F*CKWITS

A PROVEN STRATEGY TO FIND YOUR PERFECT RELATIONSHIP

By

Amanda Robinson

THE CONSCIOUS DATING COACH

Published by Amanda Robinson

Edited by Leeza Baric https://leezabaric.com
Cover and Interior Design by Ina Kuehfuss https://inawonderworld.com

The author of this book does not dispense medical advice or prescribe the use of any technique as a form of treatment for physical, emotional, or medical problems without the advice of a physician, either directly or indirectly. The intent of the author is only to offer her story and information in a general nature. In the event you use any of the information in this book for yourself, the author/publisher assumes no responsibility for your actions.

Cataloguing-in-Publication Data is on file at
Legal Deposit State Library of Queensland and the National Library of Australia.

E-book ISBN: 978-0-6455274-6-9

Tradepaper ISBN: 978-0-6455274-6-9
1st Edition June 2022

DEDICATED TO:

My partner Dan, who made my journey worthwhile. I feel that without my experiences—good and bad, the copious amounts of research and counselling, I would not have recognised you for the extraordinary person you are and we wouldn't be where we are today. Looking forward to many more amazing years with you.

To my mother who decided she wanted to raise strong, confident women. Although some may feel she overdid it, ha ha, we have fearlessly tackled life head on because of this.

CONTENTS

PREFACE

In the fairy-tale, the handsome prince comes and kisses Sleeping Beauty, although I'm pretty sure that's sexual assault. Something that will ultimately catch up with the princes of today. Then he whisks her away to a wonderful new life and they live happily ever after.

Hmm, call me cynical, but girl, this just isn't going to happen! So here's Plan B.

This book contains no BS, no gimmicks, no manifesting (although feel free to do it, it can't hurt, right?) It is strategy based. It's not about WAITING for your fairy-tale ending, it's about CREATING your own personalised fairy-tale ending. Knowing what you want in life and in a partner is crucial.

What you will get from this book:

Empowerment, knowledge and a strategy to implement to help you find your perfect partner.

How to use this book:

Read, learn, laugh, and answer the questions in this book. Writing your thoughts provides clarity. Fully commit to the process and trust in the strategy that I have tried and tested; developed through decades of dating and relationships.

I became a Dating Coach and a Counsellor because of my dating experiences. I wrote this book is to help my fellow dating sisters benefit from my many, many mistakes. It got to a point where I spent every hour researching personality disorders, mental health issues, and red flags. If they existed, I was going to know about them!

I was NEVER going to date a F*ckwit again.

I hope you can learn from my mistakes because I don't like to see women suffer or waste time. I believe that every woman deserves to be treated well and to stay sane when looking for the love of their life.

I'm with you, sister!

PS: Definition of a F*ckwit—The dictionary says F*ckwit is slang for an unpleasant or stupid person. I'll settle for that, an unpleasant idiot.

CHAPTER 1

My Story: The Good, The Bad and The Ugly

Let's begin in a cold and miserable United Kingdom (UK). I'd recently discovered that my partner had another life, a secret life that was as disturbing as it was shocking. Nothing about him added up anymore and it was never going to because I only ever knew the smallest tip of a very disquieting iceberg.

I decided to take a year off and travel to Australia alone, as you do! I'd throw caution to the wind. After all, where had planning my life so carefully ever got me? So, I threw the chips in the air and waited to see where they would fall. (By the way, this is not part of the strategy I recommend for you. It just seemed like a good idea at the time.)

My parting words to my ex as I left were, "I'm going to Australia. The moon isn't far enough away from you." Incidentally, I didn't know a single person in Australia. It felt like the ultimate fresh start.

A few weeks in, curiosity got the better of me and I went on a dating site "just to look." I instantly recognised a face staring back at me. It was the strangest thing. It felt like I knew something about him, but in reality, I didn't know anything about him. It felt like that knowledge was just beyond my grasp. *Spoiler Alert: My counsellor later said she felt he was my nemesis from a past life. Sounded a bit woo-woo to me, but with no better explanation, I'll go with that. It just about summed up the toxic rollercoaster that my life became the moment I met my husband-to-be. If I'd had the knowledge from this book back then, I would have run for the hills. More about him later.

I met lots of other F*ckwits along the way, lots of cheating F*ckwits, lying F*ckwits, all round general F*ckwits, but there was definitely the F*ckwit of all F*ckwits who should surely win a prize, F*ckwit of the year. He'd probably think that was an accolade.

This particular F*ckwit was the Psychopath F*ckwit, let's just call him PF for short. When I explained to the PF that I'd previously had an abusive relationship, he must have been rubbing his grubby little mitts together with glee. He thought he had found the perfect victim. He behaved impeccably for a few months. I was introduced to his friends and family; nothing too untoward, until one day my gut-feeling sprang into action. The feeling was so powerful in a way I just couldn't ignore.

This ultimately led me to investigate him. He fell into the trap I had laid to test him as he sat on my sofa typing away to his next date. He believed I was having a shower, but no, I was the one typing back from the bathroom. I'd created a fake account to perfectly fit his kind of woman. Of course, I hoped my gut was wrong, but it wasn't.

I was in shock and not as good at lying as he was. To explain why I was noticeably upset, I told him I was just thinking of things my ex-husband had done. He seemed to sense something was off and appeared slightly rattled, or more likely bored. I started suffering with a migraine, which was triggered by my elevated levels of stress. PF then gave me a combination of medications that really shouldn't have been used together. As a doctor, he should have been aware of this. It promptly knocked me out and when I woke the next day; he was gone.

Me being me; I drove for three hours to his home to confront him. I'll not go into the absolute load of tripe that spilled from his lying mouth, but he ran away just long enough to delete all the "evidence" from his phone and returned to readily proffer it to me along with pleas of innocence. Then he bravely ran away once more.

I switched his phone to airplane mode, should he try to interfere with it from afar. Then I plugged it into my laptop and downloaded the software that can be used to restore data that has been accidentally deleted...or otherwise. I received far more than I ever bargained for! This was no ordinary F*ckwit. This was a F*ckwit of the highest order. Again, I think he'd probably like that title, but moving on...

Let's just say by the end of my investigations, the police, the medical board, patients and ex-girlfriends were all involved. This F*ckwit was a bona fide psychopath. His ex-wife, who just happened to be a psychiatrist, confirmed this. She said, "He's a dangerous sociopath. Stay away from him." Unfortunately, he is still out there, ladies, so beware. At this point, I read every book and paper about psychopathy that was out there. Fool me once...

It's funny, but I did happen across another PF on my dating adventures, but this time I swiftly nipped him in the bud. I recognised he was more affronted that his ex decided to leave him than he was about losing his ex. He thought he might be on the autism spectrum because people said he was "different". He didn't have the same attachment to people that he noticed others had. I definitely noticed a shallow affect, showing little range in emotion.

He also told me he used to be a male stripper on stage. Oh boy. When I laughed, he said, "Fifteen thousand screaming women can't be wrong." I asked if they were screaming and running in the opposite direction.

He had the superficial charm and charisma and I felt his need for dominance, power and control. I also noticed he was very calculated and measured in so many ways. As a person,

I found him extremely intriguing, and I can see why he had no problems finding new victims. This time, I knew better. Knowledge is power, ladies.

As an intelligent woman, I knew there had to be a strategy to find here. So, using my catalogue of dating experiences, I fathomed a path through the mire that is online dating.

I discovered Attachment Theory during my time studying psychology, trying to work out where I was going wrong in the dating game. I cannot stress enough how valuable this knowledge is to anyone looking for their future partner. It is the foundation upon which every relationship is built. If the foundations are unsuitable, the cracks in the relationship will soon appear.

I created boundaries for myself and became very firm about avoiding the very handsome and charming men who were never going to eventuate to anything. Hey, it's not easy ladies, but if you are to move forward to the relationship you want, cut the ill-suited men free. Oh, they'll contact you again and tempt you off the straight and narrow. One contacted me a year to the day that I'd parted company with him for good. I'm so glad I stuck to my guns on this one because within a month, I had met Dan.

It took a long time to refine my final strategy. I realised that I wasn't being strict enough with myself. It's easy to get distracted by men who, if the truth be told, are just not that suitable. I ultimately gave myself four weeks, the go hard or go home method. Four weeks to find my perfect man. It was as we say in counselling a S.M.A.R.T. goal: Specific, Measurable, Achievable, Relevant and, most importantly for me, Time limited. I was exhausted from years of dating.

It doesn't have to be this full on, but I'd figured out by this point there had to be a numbers game element to meeting the right man. I just didn't think I could sustain more than a month of SOOO much dating without having a rest at the end. Thank God I met Dan in week three!

Dan has sailed through relationships. No dramas. No divorces. His practical, no nonsense approach hasn't left him struggling in the wake of a bad marriage. If it's not working and you can't fix it, no harm—no foul—move on, is Dan's motto.

When you strip the emotions away, that's how simple it is, but not everyone has such a cool and calm capacity to see through the complications of a bad relationship and peacefully call it a day!

Dan's quietly assured he'll always survive and that he will always meet someone else. Those of us who are a touch more anxious could benefit from being with someone who is more secure. These last few years with Dan have been the best years of my life. I never knew a relationship could be this good.

CHAPTER 2

Attachment Style and Why it's So Important

The Attachment Style is probably the most important factor you need to know about your future partner. I discovered Attachment Theory when I was researching the psychology of dating. Attachment describes our emotional bond with another person. We develop our Attachment Style from our earliest bonds with our caregivers, although this isn't always solidly set in stone and our life experiences can continue to shape our Attachment Style.

First, we need to work out what Attachment Style you are, so we can determine who you are best suited to. There are many places online where you can test your Attachment Style, most are freebies. Some are super in-depth and, in most cases, we don't need all of that extra information, but knock yourself out if you're interested in exploring further.

The simplest online Attachment Style test and the one I recommend can be found at: https://Attachedthebook.com

In my one-to-one sessions during my four-week course, this is one of the first investigations I will do with you. Although the test will give you an Attachment Style, we don't all conform that simply.

I am mostly a Secure Attachment Style and the Attached Quiz classifies me as Secure. I do, however, possess enough anxiously attached traits that I cannot date an "Avoidant". (Keep reading for this to make sense!).

I am massively triggered and unbalanced from my Secure state by Avoidants. Put me with someone like Dan, who is a "Secure" and my relationship experience is completely transformed and yours will be too!

This is why Attachment Style is so important, especially for anyone with an Anxious Attachment Style or Anxious traits. Avoidants are our nemesis, yet we are drawn together. Go figure! It's likely that we fulfil each other's expectations of what we fear in relationships. By the way, the book Attached - The Science of Adult Dating is definitely on my must read list for you. I've literally forced friends to read it because, as they do, they realise what has been happening to them and how they can change it. There's a link on my website: https://Theconsciouscounsellingcompany.com

How Attachment Styles are Formed

To simply explain, our Attachment Style comes from our experience as a baby and as a child growing up.

A SECURE ATTACHMENT happens when our caregiver/parents are:

- Available
- Responsive
- Sensitive to our needs
- Accepting of us

This leads to children who learn how to trust and have healthy levels of self-esteem. In turn, this leads to SECURE adults who are in touch with their feelings, happy with emotional closeness, competent and usually have successful relationships.

An ANXIOUS (INSECURE) ATTACHMENT happens when our caregiver/ parents are:

- Unreliable when needed
- Unresponsive when needed
- Not sensitive to our needs

This leads to a child who realises they can't rely on their parent/s. Their parent/s are not consistently available for their child and fail to meet their needs. Therefore, the child fails to develop a sense of security from that parent/s. The child can then become demanding and clingy to evoke a response from the parent/s. In turn, this leads to an ANXIOUS (INSECURE) adult who wants a lot of reassurance and closeness, and who may act up or become distressed when their needs are not met. They can feel insecure, needy, distrustful, and maybe even feel angry.

AVOIDANT (INSECURE) ATTACHMENT happens when our caregiver/ parents are:

- Not accepting of the child
- Don't respond with sensitivity
- Rejects their demands
- Won't help the child when needed

This leads to a child who has to meet their own needs and avoids asking the parent for anything, as they have proved unhelpful. This child learns to close down their feelings and to trust solely in self-reliance. This leads to an adult who feels more comfortable being self-reliant and emotional closeness is extremely difficult for them. It doesn't mean they don't want relationships, they just find it very difficult to maintain them. Too much emotional closeness will see them running for the hills. When the emotional distance has been established and they feel safe once more, they will be back in touch again. This looks like a very confusing push/pull that most of us have experienced when dating someone at some time.

DISORGANISED ATTACHMENT is rarer, but this happens when our caregiver/parents are:

- Rejecting
- Ridiculing to the child
- Frightening to the child
- Often the parents are trauma victims themselves and feel fear and anxiety when the child approaches instead of the need to care and protect

This child has DISORGANISED ATTACHMENT because there is no strategy the child can create and this results in disorganised behaviour. The child may be aggressive to the parent, refuse any care from them, or become extremely self-reliant. This can lead to an increased risk of psychopathy, trouble with self-regulation, poor coping skills, erratic behaviour and becoming volatile in relationships.

I'll do a separate section on psychopaths, as there are many more than you think out there. Thankfully, very few of them are serial killers!

So you can see how understanding the different Attachment Styles plays a massive part in steering yourself away from F*ckwits. It was the most powerful tool of them all for me due to my anxious traits.

So What Happens When different Attachment Styles Meet?

SECURES:

When SECURES date SECURES, all is well in the world. There's no drama and even if it doesn't work out for other reasons, they're not worried. Secures know there's plenty more fish in the sea.

When SECURES date ANXIOUS Styles, the solid, reliable nature of the SECURE and their comfort with emotional closeness means they can often stabilise the ANXIOUS person. This can be an excellent match for both.

When SECURES date AVOIDANTS, well, the AVOIDANT is going to run when the emotional closeness gets too much, which leads to the push/pull. It may be a tolerable match if the SECURE isn't upset by the AVOIDANT'S need for emotional distance.

ANXIOUS:

When ANXIOUS dates AVOIDANTS, here's where the trouble really starts. The ANXIOUS partner wants emotional closeness and is very sensitive to signs something may be wrong. The closer the ANXIOUS partner tries to get, the more the AVOIDANT partner pulls away. Emotional closeness is not comfortable for them and they withdraw. At this point, it is extremely triggering for the ANXIOUS partner who is confused, upset, and anxious due this response.

Once the emotional distance has been established, the AVOIDANT partner then feels the need to reach out again. They feel safer and, after all, they really liked the ANXIOUS partner. The ANXIOUS partner is relieved and doesn't understand what happened, but they are so happy to have the AVOIDANT return and thus the push/pull continues. This is very dangerous to the mental health of the ANXIOUS party, but they attract each other like moths to a flame, each reinforcing their own fears about relationships. It is an extremely toxic mix.

AVOIDANTS, well, they don't date each other. There is literally no emotional glue to hold them together!

DISORGANISED attachment will stand out more to most people, but they still do end up in relationships, often very difficult ones.

Secures make up around fifty percent of the general population, with the Anxious making up twenty-five percent and Avoidants twenty percent. The dating pool has a disproportionate amount of Avoidants compared to the general population because the Secures pass through it quickly. The Avoidants are then thrown back into the pool more often, along with anyone else who struggles with relationships. That is exactly why you need to be aware of the Attachment Styles when you enter the dating pool.

CHAPTER 3

SAVING YOURSELF:
Self-Care and Working with a Counsellor

As women, we tend to put our own needs last. Self-care is so important, especially in today's hectic world. I want you to live your best life, in whatever form gives you joy. Physically, you can exercise, do yoga, go for walks on the beach or in the park, journal, swim, have a massage, or facial, or literally do whatever floats your boat.

There are many things we can do to work on ourselves mentally and emotionally. You can read good books, hang out with friends, go to workshops or retreats or visit counsellors or healers. Counsellors can look deeper into areas you may need help with. They work WITH you to change the elements that no longer work FOR you.

You may have self-limiting thoughts or behaviours you aren't even aware of but they are sabotaging your life or preventing you from finding your perfect partner. A counsellor can help you to identify them.

How many times has our inner critic berated us harshly? Would we say those words to a friend? Working on your inner critic and replacing that b*tch with a kind and helpful inner friend can work wonders for us all.

We can only change ourselves and that's an important thing to recognise. We can all grow, flourish, and bloom when we are in the right environment. This is why it's so important to choose your partner wisely from a position of knowledge and self-empowerment.

I want you to feel empowered. Speak your truth freely and confidently, honour your worth and hold your chosen boundaries with strength.

Self-reflection is a must.

It's important to recognise things that may be holding you back and how to move past them, such as: self-limiting beliefs, behaviours that no longer serve you, and elements in your life that drain your joy.

I may be biased here, but counselling literally saved me at a time when I felt broken and defeated. My counsellor helped me to repair those broken pieces, so that I was stronger and more self-aware than ever before. I realise that not everyone is going to need it. If you think you'd benefit, it's not about how many degrees or qualifications your counsellor has but the relationship and level of rapport you have with your him or her. They should be your biggest cheerleader, recognising all your finest qualities, strengths and gifts, then helping you to bring in them to the fore.

Your counsellor should help you work on any blocks or traumas you may be struggling with. They should challenge you when they feel it would be helpful to raise your awareness and allow for growth. Giving you the practical tools to repair what is damaged and put that baggage down, girl!

The one thing I was determined to do when I left my ex-husband was to take absolutely none of his bullshit with me moving forward in my life, especially when it came to relationships. Dragging that heavy emotional baggage to your next relationship is a surefire way to help it fail. I wanted rid of it. I wanted no part of it. I would not let my ex-husband ruin my life forever, in that I was beyond determined and counselling was at the centre of my success.

I also had questions. How had one person systematically destroyed me when I was previously so strong?

My ex-husband was an odd cat. He was handsome and charming, as most abusive men are, but he operated on another level. Passive aggression was his love language. I swear it was as natural to him as breathing. My brain just wasn't wired that way.

I believed I'd never experienced passive aggression. It wasn't a language spoken where I grew up. Then my counsellor dug up memories from long ago when my father had disconnected the electricity to the stables and used to take the phone with him when he went out, so I couldn't use it. These memories had become lost in time, but I've got no doubt that it had created some kind of familiarity and comfort with that type of abuse and it had seeped into my psyche.

I described my ex-husband as relentless, but my counsellor said he's obsessive. He still sends me emails years and years later. I never opened them, and Dan helped me to block him. He's probably still sending them because that's who he is.

My counsellor said she thought he had Borderline Personality Disorder. She helped me understand my reactions to him, how he affected me so greatly, and why it made me so ill. I developed five autoimmune disorders, which incidentally went away when I left him for good. The marriage was toxic, the abuse both physical and mental grew and thank God I finally came to my senses.

I was exhausted and left with Post Traumatic Stress Disorder (PTSD). I felt broken into a million tiny pieces.

This is why I feel counselling is an important element in the course that I run for women who struggle to find their amazing life partner. It's like a First Aid kit, not always necessary, but there on hand if you need it.

We are all learning. I learned mostly the hard way, but as African-American author and poet Maya Angelou said, "When you know better, you do better."

CHAPTER 4

Creating Your Own Life – Because Who Needs Prince Charming Anyway?

Happiness is not all about the man.

What about you? Your career or business? What sort of home do you want and where? In the city, country, mountains or beach? Describe it to me. Make that vision big, bold, and bright.

Make a mood board and keep it where you can see it every day. If you don't know what a mood board is, it's simply a visual collage of pictures, notes, anything that's inspiring to you. It reminds you on a daily basis where you want to be in your future life.

ALWAYS keep your eyes on your future goals and walk boldly in that direction with every move you make and you will get there, girl!

Your future partner must fit into this plan. If you find yourself cancelling your own plans for the plans of a new partner first be sure to ask yourself, is this what I really want? If you say "absolutely" with every part of your being, then great. If you would really have rather have the life you created on your mood board, you have to make a judgement. Is the trade worth it?

I discovered that my dreams were much larger than Dan's. He just didn't expect that much from life, but I take my hat off to him. Dan has embraced every crazy idea I've had, and together we steer the ship on our journey. Talking of steering ships, Dan bravely took the wheel of our catamaran too in an unexpected storm whilst I helpfully vomited over the side and tried not to die! That's the kind of man we all need.

We have ended up in the perfect place, both metaphorically and physically, for us. I'm more country, he's more city. We have the perfect home. One side is so quiet and peaceful, directly on the water, the other side is five minutes from the city centre, near to everything we would ever need.

We have grown so much more together than either of us could have grown alone. I never knew a relationship could be like this. By sticking to my guns on what I wanted and what I didn't want, even when friends doubted me, I found the perfect man for me and so can you.

CHAPTER 5

The "Soul Mate" Trap

If you are of an Anxious Attachment Style, this fallacy of the "soul mate" will have your attachment system activated at lightning speed. You already feel that love is rare and hard to find.

We are taught to believe that we have a soul mate; one, uno, single shining star in an infinite universe. It already feels impossible, right? The truth is, there are many people on this planet that we could have a wonderful life with. We just haven't met them all yet. The sooner you can recognise them, the better.

The Scarcity Myth

There are 7.1 billion people on this earth, but if you follow the "soul mate" advice emanating from so many of the books on dating, you need to find this one endangered species in that 7.1 billion to be happy. Finding a needle in a haystack sounds easier, right?

Let's put this one to bed early.

Dating is akin to separating the wheat from the chaff, the good for you from the not so good for you. It's then a matter of finding the men with qualities that reflect your true values, needs and desires and from then on, it's a numbers game. That said, there will always be those fortunate enough to meet their ideal partner on the first or second date, like Dan did when he met me.

There will also be those like myself for whom it will be akin to panning for gold, you have to move a lot of earth and have a lot of dates to find that diamond. Friends will tell you that you'll never find anyone if you keep rejecting everyone! This simply isn't true. Those friends are projecting their own fears on to you, and this happens quite a lot when it comes to relationships. Stay true to you and what you want.

I used to make the same mistakes over and over and over and over on repeat ad nauseam. I remember years ago, in fact no, decades ago, my friend's husband saying, "Amanda has got to be picking these men. She can't have that much bad luck!" I was seriously insulted.

My immediate reaction was, "Why would I do that to myself? Can't you see I'm trying my best here?" It took years of more research and education to realise he was right. I felt comfortable with this type of person because there was a familiarity, like putting on an old pair of slippers. This can be from ex-partners or your family. We absorb, like osmosis, what happens around us growing up and we can repeat the same unhealthy dynamics some of our families and relationships have demonstrated to us.

In counselling many years later, I was told we all have hooks. Yes, hooks! Our subconscious hooks are caused by our previous experiences, our upbringing, whatever feels familiar and safe to us. So when the F*ckwit with a matching set of hooks walks past you, you hook each other! They feel comfortable with you; you feel comfortable with them. It feels familiar; you both feel at home. This is why people from abusive backgrounds go on to recreate the same; subconsciously we are choosing what is familiar.

Self-reflection and actively working on ourselves is so important. Understanding what we truly want and need, our true values, and our path to where we want to be in life is invaluable.

The Miracle Question

This is a question that I ask in counselling when a client is struggling to understand what needs to change.

Ask yourself the Miracle Question:

Tonight you go to sleep and when you wake up, you realise a miracle has happened. Suddenly everything in your life is perfect and exactly what you'd want it to be. What does your world look like?

Write down:

- What's changed?
- How do the changes make you feel?
- What's life like now that everything has changed?
- Is there a man in your life?
- Who is he and how does he make you feel?
- Are there children, pets, family, friends, career?

____

____

____

____

____

Keep it going and see how the future you design really makes you feel. This will enable you to see with clarity what you really want in life. Add it to your earlier list. It's not just about choosing a man, we can choose our whole life.

I did this and I must say, knowing what I wanted and then creating the life for myself has led me to a life and partner I really wanted, except better. I never imagined that my strategy would have led me to a partner so suitable that I had to buy him a Mr Perfect mug! No pressure Dan.

CHAPTER 6

What Do You Want in Life?

It's really important to know what you want in your life. How can you work towards your goals if they have never been defined? Do you want to feel loved, to feel peaceful and happy, to feel fulfilled, to feel alive and healthy?

I want you to write three lists:

a) A list of your values and refer to that list when you are dating:

b) A list of your non-negotiables—ten things you absolutely DON'T want in a man!

I'll give you a start:

1) Men in relationships—I don't care if they say they're going to leave their partner, or that they're just living together to save costs. (Pull the other one—it plays Jingle Bells!)

Now you create the other nine:

2) ______________________________

3) ______________________________

4) ______________________________

5) ______________________________

6) ______________________________

7) ______________________________

8) ______________________________

9) ______________________________

10) ______________________________

c) A list of what you really DO want in a man. Go wild, aim high, this is YOUR wish list. If you're itching to manifest at this point, do it!

As a counsellor, people tell me what they don't want and that works perfectly for counselling. In coaching, it's different. You're here to improve what you struggle with.

We are all flawed and all very different, but there's a lid for every pot. We have to find the perfect lid for us.

The things that will get you into trouble are, but not limited to these few:

- People pleasing
- Apologising for who you are
- Tolerating abusive/toxic people
- Negative self-talk
- Lack of self-worth
- Choosing the wrong man rather than being alone
- Doing the same thing over and over again hoping to get a different result
- Rushing headlong into a new relationship, moving in/getting married/pregnant too soon. Remember, time is your friend. "Marry in haste—repent at leisure" as my mother used to say!

I want you to look for the type of man who will be your rock when things get tough. I also don't want you to try to "fix" anyone. The birds with broken wings, they heal and then they fly away or worse, you spend the rest of your life rescuing them. Look for an equal, not a saviour or a broken bird. Rescue a dog if you want to fill that need. Dogs are the best!

When you are dating, refer to your three lists often. Remember what you wanted and don't get pulled off course by a hot man, ladies. I don't care if he's a firefighter!

CHAPTER 7

Anxiety Around Dating

Let's face it, who hasn't felt anxious around dating? As a counsellor, I help people to deal with anxiety about anything and everything.

Symptoms of anxiety can include:

- Butterflies or a churning stomach
- A rapid heartbeat
- Shortness of breath
- Feeling lightheaded or dizzy
- Trembling or shaking
- Sweating
- Your voice may quiver
- You can feel apprehensive, your mind may race, making it difficult to concentrate. This can make it hard to stay present on dates and be yourself, which leads to a lack of connection with your date
- You may find excuses to cancel dates or not agree to them

One important thing to remember is that your date is likely to be nervous too. I know Dan was. He said his friends thought he was so incapable that they wanted to escort him. They'd already berated him for ordering a milkshake on the first date he went on.

If you are caught out in the moment, grounding techniques can help, such as using the 54321 game to ground yourself.

How to use the 54321 Grounding Game:

1. Name 5 things you can see (you can do this in your head)
2. Name 4 things you can feel (a glass, a chair, the ground under your feet, etc)
3. Name 3 things you can hear (birds chirping, traffic noise, a baby crying, etc)
4. Name 2 things you can smell
5. Name 1 thing you like about yourself

You can also use long, slow breaths in through your nose and out through your mouth. Chewing and smiling also help. These things give feedback from the body to the brain that all is well and help to calm the nervous system.

Emotional Freedom Technique

One of my favourite ways of dealing with anxiety both for myself and for my clients is Emotional Freedom Technique (EFT). It's better to prepare to calm yourself in advance if you feel you have anxiety around dating. EFT is a great way to address what bothers you most and to put that anxiety to bed long before those dates.

EFT is sometimes called Tapping. Together with my client, we write a list of the things that cause them the most anxiety and what they dislike about those things. It works best when it's personalised. We then repeat the phrases whilst tapping with our finger/s on specific meridian points of the head, face and body. These are some of the same points that are used in acupuncture.

The tapping helps to deactivate the amygdala. The amygdala is part of the limbic system in our brain and plays a key role in responding to threat by processing the emotions and memories associated with fear.

I use several rounds of EFT as it effectively peels away layers like peeling an onion and we continue to tap on what comes up for my client. Often the anxiety is linked to something deeper and by repeating the technique we can identify that cause and deactivate the amygdala's response to it. It even works on skeptics. I know because I was one. I like it because it works quickly. In just one session we can go from a highly anxious state to "why was I so worried about that again?"

There are many other modalities that also work for anxiety, but this one is my stand out because the results are so great. It's also my preferred choice when helping clients with all kinds of dating anxieties or self-esteem issues on both my dating course and in my counselling sessions. Yay for EFT!

CHAPTER 8

Myths:
You'll Never Be Happy Alone and The Perfect Partner

Ah, yet another myth we are sold. That you'll never be happy until you're happy alone.

As humans, for thousands of years we have survived by depending on others, whole villages of others. Now we are told to defy these inherent traits and simply everyone MUST be one-hundred percent happy with going it alone before they can be happy with a partner. That is simply not the case. We didn't evolve this way. We have a need to have human connection and having it makes us feel safer in the world. Forcing yourself to try and be happy alone goes against thousands of years of human development, so don't beat yourself up if you feel happier with a partner.

For a few, yes! Avoidants feel more comfortable with a safe emotional distance, but even they want relationships.

Accept who you are, don't try to force yourself to be something you simply are not or feel guilty that you have needs. So many people are happier and more content in a good relationship, so embrace and be who you are. Don't try to mould yourself into someone else's idea of what you should be. You're perfect just the way you are.

Talking of villages, there's another myth I want to address. The myth that one man has to be everything for you. This poor man has to be capable of playing the part that a whole village used to play! It doesn't mean you should ignore what is important to you, you should always strive for what you need in a relationship. Just be sure to check in with yourself when you're about to drop the latest guy because he doesn't like yoga (or whatever floats your boat). Who else could fulfil that need? Do you really need him to be that thing in your life if someone else in your circle is a perfect replacement?

Bless Dan, he's tried many of my interests even though a few have nearly killed him, naming no names of local mountains. Despite his near-death experiences, he does still enjoy some of them.

He even tried Reformer Pilates, but it didn't float his boat. I tried his gym, but my former back surgery decided that was a definite no. He plays volleyball; I don't. I swear my arms would snap and don't tell him, but I'm getting him tennis lessons for his birthday as my leaping around days are gone.

CHAPTER 9

Giving Up

A comfort zone is where dreams go to die.

Are you someone who seems to have given up, having chosen a safe, single life over any chance of another bad relationship?

When life is safe, easy and comfortable, changing that can seem counter-intuitive. Let me tell you straight, you can't make an omelette without breaking eggs. To get what we want in life will probably mean putting on our big girl pants and stepping outside that comfort zone.

Some may simply prefer to go through life alone. Avoidants may seem strong, as if they prefer to be alone, but mistrust and fear may lie at the heart of that shield. Never allowing themselves to get too close to or rely on anyone.

We all are entitled to our own choices in life, and if being alone is the perfect choice for you, I respect that.

If you are alone through fear, anxiety or trauma, this can feel like you have no other choice. Fear is very powerful. This is where the help of a great counsellor can be invaluable. To have a trusted professional walk by your side and help you navigate this journey can free you from your fear and comfort zone captivity.

I hear many stories, as a counsellor, of how fear and anxiety have controlled lives, and it's heartbreaking. Anxiety makes your world smaller and prevents you from living your dreams. It doesn't have to be this way. Don't be stuck in a life you don't want to live for any longer than possible. We are not our fears, and with help, we can overcome them. I know from lived experience you can come out of trauma a stronger, more courageous, less fearful you.

CHAPTER 10

Your Dating Profile

Now we get to the nitty-gritty.

Your profile should reflect you, the real authentic you that your future partner will know six months into the relationship.

You should definitely make it clear what you want. That way, those who don't fulfil the criteria get fair warning. *A note of caution here: some F*ckwits will pretend they want what you want just to get into your knickers!

Here is a good indication that he's following your lead and saying all the things he thinks you want to hear: He asks you questions, and when you give your answers he says, "Yeah, me too".

To prevent this, you take the lead, put the ball firmly in his court and ask the questions. If he hasn't got an opinion of his own, it's a good indication that he's pretending.

I remember saying to the ex-partner of the psychopath I had dated, "What would he say if you asked him if he wanted a cup of tea or a cup of coffee?" She said, "Whatever you're having," and we both fell about laughing. He never had an opinion because he was playing a part.

If you want to have children, say it in your profile. The only men you'll scare off are the men who DON'T want them and you'll attract the ones who do. Perfect. If your pets are your life, put them in your profile.

Photo's...hmm, we've all been on a date and struggled to recognise the person in the profile. Put up your nice but realistic pics. Once again, you'll attract the person who really likes you.

A very important point here, bait your hook according to what you want to catch. If your pics are showing off lots of boobs and butt, you'll likely catch a F*ckwit on the end of your line. Be tasteful and reflective of who you are. I used lots of sporty pictures as yet again, another reminder that he'd better be active. I may also have written "Unless you're very active, you'll only be able to see me through binoculars, in the distance, up a mountain! Hint-hint."

I was also clear about the age I was willing to date. I gave it five years either way. I also said, "I don't want anyone over fifty, because I hear all the good bits fall off after fifty!" I received so much stick for that one. Karma also bit me firmly on the bum when a part of my spine fell off on my fiftieth birthday!

Be you, in whatever fabulous form that is. Don't try to be someone you are not, as you won't attract the amazing match you want.

Most of the dating sites let you choose your parameters. Use these to filter out anyone you definitely don't want. I used mine to weed out the Avoidants who I know I don't play well with. I did this by setting parameters for previous relationships to a minimum of four years. Most Avoidants don't make it that far before diving back in the dating pool. Remember, those who are Secure and balanced don't stay in the dating pool for long. Avoidants are quickly back in the pool, so although they make up less than a quarter of the population, there's a much higher number to be found in the dating pool, so you'll need your wits about you!

CHAPTER 11

It's a Numbers Game

Another thing I discovered is you need to have lots and lots of dates!

Two reasons: The more people you meet, the more likely you are to meet someone great, and as a bonus, it stops you focussing and getting too involved with one person, which is a rookie error.

Date lots, "go hard or go home" is your new dating motto. Talk to lots of men online so you don't get caught up with one. Don't spend too long chatting online. It will be awkwardly embarrassing when you've spent six weeks getting super close and telling each other all your secrets only to meet up and realise that he's really not for you. Cringe.

Short coffee dates in the day are ideal. If you don't like him sober and in daylight, he needs to be crossed off the list early. The more dates you have, the more confident you will feel and the less importance you will put on it working out with the only person you've been talking to.

Just remember to take your brain (and gut) with you on these dates. There are plenty of good-looking, charming men out there who will distract you and waste your time. Work out his Attachment Style, generally dating history will give it away. Stopping these men distracting me is what led me to meeting Dan. I cut them free out of my dating life.

I thanked the men who were honest about not wanting a relationship, then I cut them free, too. Write on your profile that you only want a serious relationship if that's what you want. To stop temptation, you can hide your profile and send messages to those who fit the bill, at least in the interview stages.

I also adopted a slightly odd attitude towards my dating. In another life, I used to buy horses. I'd see these wonderful photos and great descriptions only to drive miles to find a lame duck or something equally disappointing. I always went on dates not expecting too much, then when you do meet someone who captures your interest, it's a great bonus. On the more disappointing dates, you didn't expect too much anyway, and you'd planned to catch up with a friend after for coffee! You'll also need Wing-woman, but more on that later.

CHAPTER 12

Spotting a Catfish

I'll be honest, I created one or two catfish profiles myself to test the accuracy of my gut feelings when dating suspected F*ckwits. That's a lie, it was actually three. I also caught three out of three. I told you the gut was accurate!

I learned by doing this that a smart person can create a fake account that is seamless. That said, most are created by F*ckwits and are super easy to spot. Generally, if they seem too good to be true, they are. For example:

- His photo and age don't match
- He's a lawyer but can't spell. You get the gist
- He's overseas, needs money, his family member, friend, or himself have been in an accident...blah blah blah

All total F*ckwits.

Professional pics are a giveaway, always reverse image search them. There are plenty of free Apps where you can do this. A reverse image search is used to identify if a specific photo is being used elsewhere on the internet.

You can copy and paste the image into Google Images Search or use an App on your phone.

There will be plenty to choose from if you search "reverse image search" in the App store. For example: A man calling himself John sends me a message on a dating App. I want to check to see if that is really John. I screenshot John's photographs and put them through a reverse image search App. If the photo shows up in other places, I can click on each link and see what other information that leads to.

Let's say that John's photo shows up on another type of social media with the name Mark. John either is lying about his real name or he's lying about who he is. At this point, I'd be asking John if that's his real name. I called myself after my dead dog online, a lot of people do use different names and it's not always a red flag! What is a red flag is if John says that's his real name, then you know John is lying. Deleting John would be the appropriate response here.

If the photo is of a model or it's just a professional photo available online, the chances are it's not who you are talking to. This is where you need to hone your inner Sherlock Holmes and again trust that gut. Get on his Facebook, Instagram, or other social media accounts. Do your due diligence girl and go digging. Just don't accidentally like any of his pics!

If you do want to investigate further, ask for a video chat and watch the excuses start flowing. "My camera doesn't work. I'm at work at the moment." Lies, lies and more lies. Cut your losses and run, girl!

CHAPTER 13

Psychopaths, Narcissists and Other Personality Disorders

Psychopaths

It looks dramatic, doesn't it? To see psychopaths as a headline to a chapter, but I guarantee you, they are out there and boy; they are difficult to spot. They have a gift for hiding in plain sight, their charm—a great disguise for the ruthless manipulator that lies beneath. Surprisingly, they are more common than most of us think, about one percent, so one in every one-hundred of the population.

They will usually come across as very likeable and charming. Beware of that insincere charm, it hides a master manipulator. They are naturally confident and usually have a stable job with relative success. They gravitate to higher positions, such as Chief Executive Officers (CEOs), surgeons, lawyers, doctors, and so on. They generally have higher levels of intelligence. Their inflated sense of self is usually well hidden, but make no mistake, they'll stomp on anyone who gets in their way.

Psychopaths are impulsive and self-centred. Cheating with a high level of promiscuity, lying and stealing are just the tip of the iceberg. They quietly break rules, and they loathe authority. They don't feel guilt, empathy or remorse, but will feign it. They will endeavour to gain your pity by playing the victim.

So how did I spot the psychopath I had the misfortune to date? My gut. I've never had such a strong gut reaction to anything. Psychopaths do have weaknesses. They find it impossible to see the bigger picture, or how one lie may interact with another. They simply can't keep track and this is often what trips them up.

For example, when I saw the horrifying things on the PF's phone that he'd willingly handed over to me, I knew one person who would be able to answer many of the questions that I now had. PF had spent copious amounts of time explaining he was the victim of his ex-partner.

I knew her name. I knew where she worked and I knew where she lived because PF had searched the house they used to live in online and shown it to me. One of the first things I did was drive to her home. I ding-donged the bell at the closed gates and a young man came outside, who I presumed to be her son. He told me she wasn't in, so I asked if I could leave a note for her.

What I didn't know was that her son innocently placed my handwritten note on her bedside table without explanation. When she read it, she immediately thought I'd broken into her home and left it there. A wild assumption you may think until you learn that PF had quite recently broken into her house in the middle of the night and she woke up in the dark to find him standing over her!

If you knew that you were deliberately faking a relationship to get joy out of screwing someone over, the last thing you would do is to give them the actual information. Oh no, not the self-assured psychopath, because he can't see beyond the end of his nose.

Narcissists

Narcissists have a grandiose sense of self-importance and exaggerate their talents and achievements, dreaming of unlimited power, success or love. They believe they are special and only other special people can understand them. Requiring a lot of admiration, they will exploit others for personal gains and expect extra special treatment. One word to describe them is—arrogance!

Dating is all about the art of the game. Lying, gaslighting, cheating, and financial exploitation are all part of their game, so beware. If you have a parent who is a narcissist, you are more susceptible to falling for one because it feels familiar.

I have a friend who had a relationship with a narcissist. They met whilst he was still married and began an affair. She fell pregnant, and he persuaded her to have a termination. What he failed to tell her was that his wife fell pregnant at the same time and she kept the baby. Over a decade later, he still denies that the child is his and yet my friend knows it's his child. This is just a tiny window into the twisted world of the narcissist. Unfortunately for my friend, she continued the relationship and had his children. Then he had an affair with someone else, moved in and married the next victim. He is still controlling and mentally abusing her and his children many years later.

Borderline Personality Disorder

I think I've dated the whole set, but unfortunately, this is the one I married. *Facepalm! They can be very charming and they may idealise you like you're the greatest person alive, but when it turns, you are often seen as the worst.

Borderline Personality Disorder is characterised by unregulated emotions. From one day to the next, you'll never know what's coming next. They have a deep fear of abandonment. In my case, this turned into coercive control, mental and physical abuse.

People with this disorder are intensely reactive to things that most people would just brush off. They feel empty and anger is their most common emotion. Often paranoid, they act impulsively and in self damaging ways.

My ex-husband showed signs early on. He had huge overreactions to random things. I should have seen the red flags but my head was firmly in the sand.

There are many other personality disorders that I simply don't have the scope to go into. My advice is, if you see an unusual pattern of behaviour in a potential partner, look deeper, do some research, ask more questions, but please don't bury your head in the sand. As I discovered, you can pay a high price.

CHAPTER 14

Recognising Red Flags and Trusting Your Gut

Now red flags come in all shapes and sizes and I will admit, I've probably seen and dismissed most of them. We are brainwashed to give people the benefit of the doubt. This saying should be burned at the stake.

Thankfully Maya Angelou has a much better one to offer, "When someone shows you who they are, believe them the first time." Well Maya, I just wish you'd mentioned that earlier.

People who have never dated an unsuitable man don't realise is just how charming these F*ckwits really are. It's like they all went to the same charm school and came out with doctorates in BS.

In abusive relationships, we cling to the hope that the charming, kind man we met will return. He does, just regularly enough to give you hope he may change forever, but it never lasts. If you see any of these symptoms in your relationship, get out and get out fast. Cycling through good/bad behaviour only gets more extreme as time goes on, so run!

The Lying F*ckwit

To be a good liar, you need to have a great memory and even one of the most intelligent liars I ever dated couldn't keep up with his own lies.

If you've told him something very significant, but he seems to not remember, take note and proceed with caution. I remember telling the PF that my mother had suffered a huge brain haemorrhage, and we had an in-depth discussion about how miraculous it was that she survived. This should have been all the more memorable because PF was a neurosurgeon before he was kicked out for being a F*ckwit. A couple of weeks later, PF couldn't recall this conversation. I remember thinking "Hmmm" and not being really sure what to make of it. PF was involved with that many women. He literally could not keep track of all their stories. Another red flag I should have noted.

They try to sell you on the integrity of their answers using phrases such as "to tell the truth" or "to be honest." They can also dramatise even more with sayings such as, "As God is my witness" and they swear on many lives along the way!

There are multiple signs of body language such as covering their mouth when speaking, hiding the hands, smiling exclusively with the mouth, the eyes not joining in...I could go on and on but what will probably tell you more than I ever could is—your gut. Don't let your logical brain outweigh your gut feelings. Gut feelings are there for a reason. My gut, in hindsight, has never been wrong. I just didn't know that my logical brain was less reliable. Never doubt your gut.

Coercive Control, better known as the Controlling F*ckwit

It usually starts subtly, then escalates and, like the frog in the slowly heating pot, you kind of don't notice the problem much at the start.

Here are some things this F*ckwit may say or do:

- He doesn't like what you wear... "don't you think that skirt is a bit too short?"
- He doesn't like other men looking at you; he exhibits jealousy
- He doesn't like your friends, maybe even family; he may say they are a bad influence on you
- He wants to spend all his time with you. Don't feel flattered, he wants to isolate you from friends and family so that he can control you
- He'll call when you are out with friends or staying late at work, puts pressure on you to come home, questioning what you are doing
- He's charmingly insistent; he'll say he only wants the best for you
- He may be jealous of your exes. He thinks he's right about everything
- He eventually won't be happy just controlling your life, body, and actions. He will do his best to control your thoughts and emotions too
- He will constantly criticise you
- He will push you to change things about yourself
- He will blame you for everything, turn the tables and never admit mistakes

This F*ckwit can literally make you feel like you are losing your mind.

Controlling F*ckwits are very insecure about themselves and deep down, he knows that he doesn't deserve you. Rather than change himself, he will try to control you. Your loyalty will be questioned. He doesn't want you to have any privacy. He is abusive both psychologically and emotionally. Don't underestimate how toxic this can be. Ultimately, when he can't control you, he may become physically abusive.

This is what coercive control looks like.

F*ckwit Red Flags:

- He has no friends
- He calls exes crazy
- He has a history of infidelity
- Has a lack of empathy
- He minimises bad behaviour
- He Gaslights you: "I never said that," and/or "that never happened"

Never downplay this behaviour, he's a danger to your mental health.

F*ckwit Abuse comes in many forms:

- Physical abuse, such as pushing, restraining you, hitting or physically harming you in any way
- Verbal abuse, such as name calling, bullying, accusing, minimisation, threatening, yelling at you, belittling you, scolding, labelling or harassing you. Manipulative language, denigrates your self-improvement
- Financial abuse, such as restricting or controlling your access to money, refusing to contribute financially, denying access to phone, internet, transport, work or study. Running up debts in your name or pressuring you to sign a loan
- Sexual abuse, such as any sexual contact or behaviour without your willing consent. Taking explicit photos of you, denying you protection against sexual disease, taking advantage of you whilst you are under the influence of drink or drugs, forcing you into unwanted, painful or degrading sexual acts, threatening to break up if you refuse sex
- Mental and Emotional abuse, such as talking down to you, back-handed compliments, and constantly checking where you are. Gaslighting you—they may

deny something happening that you clearly remember causing a destabilised sense of solidity and competence. Confusing behaviour. Abuser blames you as the source of their problems. Abuser seeks to control and dominate you, isolates you from friends and family, and stonewalls you—the silent treatment. Passive aggressive towards you. Jealous and controlling. Unpredictable. Withholds affection or intimacy

Boundaries:

You set your own rules, that's the easy bit. Maintaining strong boundaries is where most people struggle. If someone pushes at your boundaries, it's a red flag. Pay closer attention. If someone tramples all over them, it's a deal breaker.

Respect:

Respect isn't optional. It SHOULD be a given, but as we know too well, with all the best intentions in the world, respect can be eroded. If he speaks to you with disrespect, this is a HUGE red flag. Set your values high and maintain them, put it on your values list.

Remember, we choose what we accept.

CHAPTER 15

Are You Ready for a Healthy Relationship?

Unless we are ready to accept what a great relationship looks like, we are not ready for one.

Qualities of a Good Relationship:

- There is a high level of mutual respect
- You will feel seen, heard, understood, and appreciated
- You will experience mutual growth
- You will prosper emotionally
- You will be each other's biggest fan and advocate
- You'll share values and future life hopes and dreams, whilst creating new hopes and dreams together
- You grow as individuals and as a couple and support each other in every way
- There will be a high level if consistency

Many people go through such drama in their relationships; the push-pull, heightened tensions and emotions, the triggering, arguing, and cycling through the same exhausting soul-destroying patterns. Are you willing to let all that go?

In my twenties, I was hooked on a completely dysfunctional relationship with a man who was unavailable and had more problems than he had brain cells due to the illicit substances he liked to take. Even though I was completely against drugs at the time, I wouldn't look twice at a stable, well-balanced man because they were nowhere near exciting enough for me. I wouldn't have known what to do with one and I appreciate that many people are not ready for a serious relationship when they are young.

This man or "nice guy" you'd have rejected in your twenties for feeling too safe and boring would have been wasted, their value going unrecognised. Now you recognise that they are the amazing Secures of the world. We need to evolve and grow for them to be our ideal partner.

The problems begin with the "bad guys" when you try to make this "fun but dysfunctional" relationship into a long-lasting, stable partnership, as many have tried. It's a disaster and you have definitely picked the wrong "tool" for the job. Thankfully I can look back, shake my head and laugh about it now.

Ask yourself these questions:

How would it feel to be in a relationship that was calm and consistent?

How would it feel to be fully supported by your partner in every part of your life?

How would it feel to have that intimacy, affection, and reliability without any conditions attached?

Are you at the point where you don't want to save anyone or be saved? Explain:

Are you ready to put in the work to fully understand yourself and your own needs? Why?

Are you ready to build a relationship on strong foundations? Why?

The reason I ask if you are ready, is because I know that in my twenties I certainly wasn't ready. Oh, the drama! I loved every minute of it at the time. Dan would have been wasted in my twenties. He would have been too predictable for me, nowhere near crazy enough!

Then we grow up and recognise that the guy we wouldn't have resonated with at all in our twenties was, in fact, a diamond hiding in plain sight. We need to evolve and be ready to receive what a healthy relationship has to offer.

I don't think Dan and I have ever had an argument. This is in stark contrast to my marriage to a F*ckwit who did everything within his ability to destabilise my world and bring me down to his level of misery. This example of my polar opposite relationship experiences demonstrates the importance of the strategies within this book.

If I had known then what I know now, I would have made very different decisions. It has been an absolute pleasure to have a relationship with Dan over the last few years, and he feels the same. We have enhanced each other's lives, even throughout our most difficult experiences, and we've had them!

This is how life changing this knowledge can be. Do the work on yourself, stay on your path and complete your journey to where you want to be in life.

CHAPTER 16

Heart Versus Head and Why the Gut Always Wins

I always say follow your heart but take your brain with you, but this isn't strictly true. Perhaps a more accurate phrase would end with "take your gut with you!" My gut has never been wrong, but have I always listened? The honest answer is definitely "No!"

I remember having such strong gut feelings about something being VERY wrong in my relationship with what turned out to be the Psychopathic F*ckwit. I did warn you; I used to be flypaper for freaks!

My gut was metaphorically shaking me by the shoulders, having dropped one or two, mostly ignored subtle hints. "Wake up, wake up," my gut shouted, but my brain said, "Amanda, this guy is the sweetest, nicest, kindest, most thoughtful man you've ever met...I think you are cracking up!" Notice how I went straight to blaming myself?

I distinctly remember discussing my dilemma with my mother. My mother said, "Are you sure you want to know?" I nearly spat my drink out. Her comment brought me to my senses. Of course I wanted to know!

I took matters into my own hands and thoroughly investigated the man I was dating. Can of worms doesn't quite cover the extent of what I discovered. He was dangerous, a cheat, a liar and oh, so much worse. He was a psychopath with an impeccable act. When my logical brain had failed me, my gut saw through the whole act.

I'll never forget listening to the poor girl in the United States who was kept as a sex slave in a box under a bed for years. She had hitched a lift with a seemingly normal couple. When they had stopped for fuel in a service station, she went to the bathroom. She suddenly felt a strong gut feeling that she should run, get out of there and not continue the journey with them. Her logical brain told her that would be very rude. She was being silly; they were a lovely couple, so she got back in the car. She paid a high price for her decision because she was lucky to survive. If that doesn't scare you into trusting your gut, I don't know what will!

CHAPTER 17

A Toxic Match

A toxic match such as Avoidant and Anxious partners will never run smoothly. You both reinforce your own fears. The Avoidant believes you will smother him with emotional closeness, the Anxious fears that they will be abandoned. They constantly trigger each other's individual fears. Alarm bells will go off left, right and centre.

Relationships really do take two to tango. When my previous partner and I went to couples counselling, I said, "I never start these things, but I feel I add fuel to the fire. I'm a strong character and never react well with anyone controlling."

I even said to my ex-husband, "Why on earth would you pick me if you wanted to control someone? I'm literally the worst person to try and control." Despite this, he was relentless, and he wrecked my mental and physical health. This is why I'm going to make a very important point here and I want you to take note:

Loving someone is never a good reason to stay in a bad relationship.

We are brainwashed from day one with romantic fairy-tales and movies to believe that loving someone means we should stay with them, and it is simply not true. Yes, opposites really do attract, but then they drive each other insane.

Getting the Attachment Style right is the minimum you need to form a healthy relationship. It is the foundation upon which all relationships are built. Get this part wrong at your peril! Whatever you build will crash and burn in time if the foundations are inadequate.

A good relationship is easy. Given my history, I didn't think any relationship would be easy, but once you know the essential ingredients needed to create a great relationship, you'll soon have a relationship better than you could have ever previously imagined.

If either of you is having to lose yourself to try and get the metaphorical square peg in the round hole, forget it, he's just not your penguin.

CHAPTER 18

Be Safe, Not Sorry!

I know you're not twelve, but...it just wouldn't feel right when talking about dating, not to mention safety.

A Wing-Woman or Wing-Man is Essential. A Wing-Woman is like a Wing-Man, but better. They help support or assist a friend with dating.

ALWAYS tell someone where you are going and who you are going with. Share details of your date with your Wing-woman: pics, his number, where you're meeting, the time of the meeting, and the time you'll be home.

When you plan to meet your date, email the details back to yourself. Screenshot the profiles from the dating site. Include name, all profile pictures, his telephone number and details you have, just in case...

Park your car in a public place that is well lit. I once had a friend call when I was driving to a date saying she had a bad feeling about it and asked that I not park in the underground carpark I was heading for. I said I'd had a bit of an odd feeling too, so I parked on the main road, quite close to the meeting point.

This turned out to be a bit of a lifesaver when my date decided to pick me up off the ground and try to walk off with me. Even though I was in a bit of trouble at this point, I managed to get him to put me down long enough to get into my vehicle and lock the doors. I've never been so pleased to be parked in a public place. It was even worth the parking ticket!

Make sure that you meet in a public place such as a café with lots of people around and always meet in the day until you get to know your date better.

The Escape Plan

If you struggle with escaping from bad dates, have a plan to nip to the loo and text your Wing-woman. She can then send that text or call telling you there's a reason why you need to leave immediately.

This might all seem over-cautious, but trust me, there are Dangerous F*wits out there and don't want to meet them in a dark alley!

CHAPTER 19

How WILL I Know When I Meet My Perfect Partner?

Well, you won't, not just yet, because your perfect partner has to pass the test of time. No shortcuts here, ladies!

Time is your friend, so don't do anything in a rush. The man who wants to rush you up the aisle may seem romantic, but that is another red flag. It's a sign of hidden jealousy and insecurity that is seen with coercive control.

It may also lead to the "Bait and Switch" technique. Once you are married and "belong to him", you will see the real Controlling F*ckwit show himself. A well-balanced man does not need to rush anything, after all, you are still getting to know each other.

Trust me when I say it's definitely worth the wait! My friends told me over and over "you'll never meet anyone because you keep getting rid of them", passing on their own anxieties to me.

Just before I'd met Dan, I was dating another guy for a few weeks. Nice guy, we got on well, lovely person. He was definitely a SECURE, and we laughed our heads off most of the time, but ONE thing did not resonate with me at all. He seemed to be a people pleaser, which in itself is not a crime, but this led him to telling little white lies to appease people, including me.

Lying is one of my non negotiables. Telling the truth is one of my major values. I could have carried on with this relationship and eventually it would have driven me insane. Instead, I ended it, bump, done, not for me. Within three weeks, I'd met Dan. IF I hadn't followed my own rules, I would definitely have not met Dan!

My first date with Dan got off to a slightly rocky start when he cancelled it! We were supposed to meet on Friday, so I carried on with a full weekend of speed dating and an extra couple of dates thrown in for good measure. When Dan contacted me the following week to rearrange the date, he asked what I'd been up to at the weekend. I replied that I'd been on seven dates! He said that he'd better hurry up and meet me then.

We met on Friday the 13th. He was good looking, had a great accent and a killer smile that just melted me! You see, your perfect man doesn't have to be dull. The one thing I noticed about him was he resonated calm. He didn't play games; he was interested and let it show.

The only thing I worried about initially was that he was perhaps a little too quiet for me? I'm so glad I hung around long enough for him to come out of his shell. He is hilarious with a wicked sense of humour.

He had a Secure Attachment Style and only triggered me once early on when he wouldn't post anything about us on Facebook. Now this had been a common theme amongst men who were players in my experience. Once he saw how triggered I was, he worked out how to accept the tag because it was a big deal to me, but not to him.

You see how someone secure can alleviate your anxieties? I now know that he hardly ever goes on Facebook and when he does go on, I normally grab his phone and accept all my tags that have been queued up for months. He's hopeless!

Dan has never had a dating drama, ever. He is measured and steady in his responses, so logical and practical about dating and relationships. I was his second date since he'd been back on the dating market. It just seems too easy for some people!

I honestly didn't think that a relationship could be as good as ours. We are a team; we get on like best friends. I never get bored with his company and together we have both prospered and grown. We both ended up in hospital unexpectedly having emergency surgeries, so we have definitely been tested along the way.

There's absolutely no one else I would want by my side. Only time could prove this to me. Time is your friend, so don't rush into anything.

CHAPTER 20

The Ending that Brings You New Beginnings

I may not have been able to save all the women the psychopath I dated went on to date/marry/date because that's what psychopaths do. If by writing this book, I can arm you with the necessary information to recognise men like him and kick them to the curb (or in the nuts, your choice), before they destroy your world, then I'll have achieved my goal.

We really should be taught this stuff in schools. It would surely be more helpful than trigonometry!

At this point, I look back and say to myself, what a bloody rollercoaster ride. I went through a lot to learn all of this.

I truly hope my knowledge gained from my years, let's be honest, DECADES of dating F*ckwits will help you not to!

SOOO, my dating sisters, be brave, be confident and remember you deserve the best.

You rock!

Let's Connect!

I'd love to hear about your dating stories.

Please email them to: Amanda@theconsciouscounsellingcompany.com.

Or, you can visit my website https://theconsciouscounsellingcompany.com for more information about counselling or the dating course I run for women.

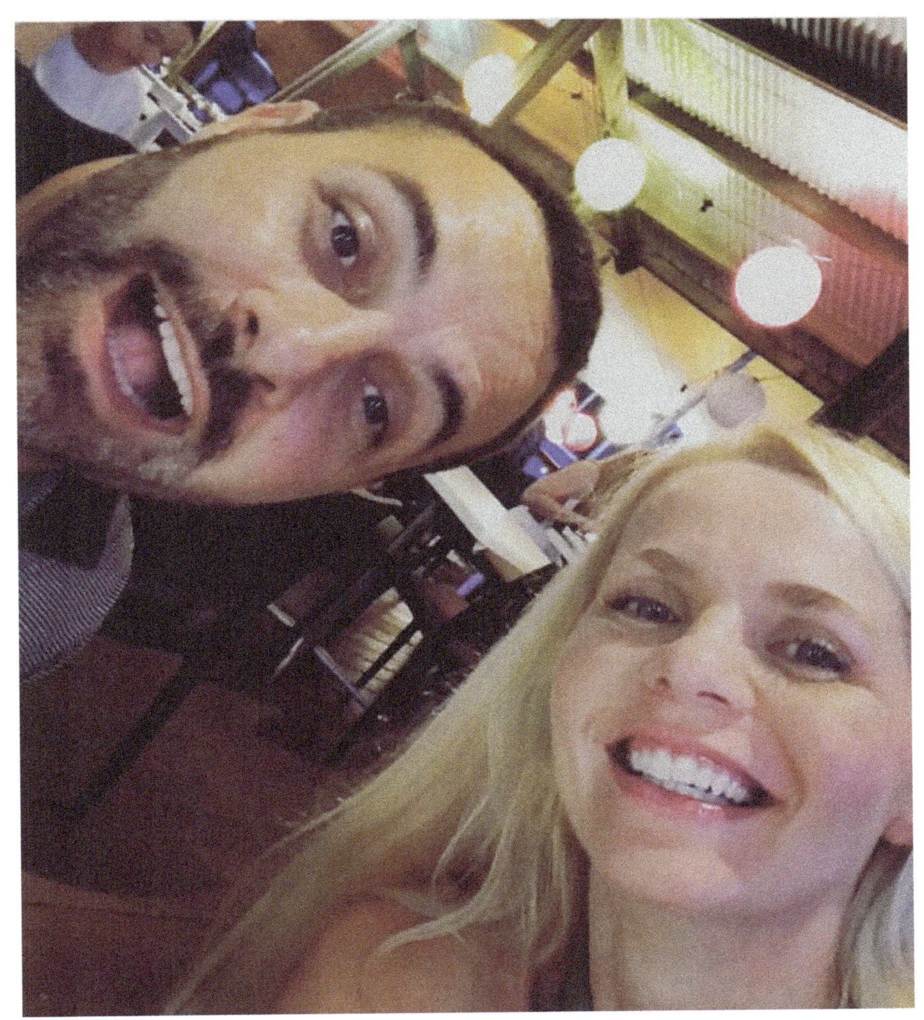

PREVIOUS RELATIONSHIPS – WORKSHEET

Think about your previous relationship:

Describe who you thought this person was and the start of the relationship:

Describe any red flags with approximate timelines and how you reacted / felt/ how long the relationship continued after and why you continued the relationship:

Describe how and why it ended and how you felt/ feel now:

PREVIOUS RELATIONSHIPS - WORKSHEET

Think about your previous relationship:

Describe who you thought this person was and the start of the relationship:

Describe any red flags with approximate timelines and how you reacted / felt/ how long the relationship continued after and why you continued the relationship:

Describe how and why it ended and how you felt/ feel now:

PREVIOUS RELATIONSHIPS – WORKSHEET

Think about your previous relationship:

Describe who you thought this person was and the start of the relationship:

Describe any red flags with approximate timelines and how you reacted / felt/ how long the relationship continued after and why you continued the relationship:

Describe how and why it ended and how you felt/ feel now:

PREVIOUS RELATIONSHIPS – WORKSHEET

Think about your previous relationship.

Describe who you thought this person was and the start of the relationship:

Describe any red flags with approximate timelines and how you reacted / felt/ how long the relationship continued after and why you continued the relationship:

Describe how and why it ended and how you felt/ feel now:

PREVIOUS RELATIONSHIPS – WORKSHEET

Think about your previous relationship.

Describe who you thought this person was and the start of the relationship:

Describe any red flags with approximate timelines and how you reacted / felt/ how long the relationship continued after and why you continued the relationship:

Describe how and why it ended and how you felt/ feel now:

DATING WORKSHEET

 **DATE 1 - Think about your recent date.**

Describe why you chose to date this person:

Describe your date, how you felt, gut feelings, red flags:

Describe how you feel after your date about this person - both positives and any concerns:

How does this person align with my values, wants and needs, future plans and non-negotiables?

DATING WORKSHEET

DATE 2 - Think about your recent date.

Describe why you chose to date this person:

Describe your date, how you felt, gut feelings, red flags:

Describe how you feel after your date about this person - both positives and any concerns:

How does this person align with my values, wants and needs, future plans and non-negotiables?

DATING WORKSHEET

DATE 3 - Think about your recent date.

Describe why you chose to date this person:

Describe your date, how you felt, gut feelings, red flags:

Describe how you feel after your date about this person - both positives and any concerns:

How does this person align with my values, wants and needs, future plans and non-negotiables?

DATING WORKSHEET

DATE 4 - Think about your recent date.

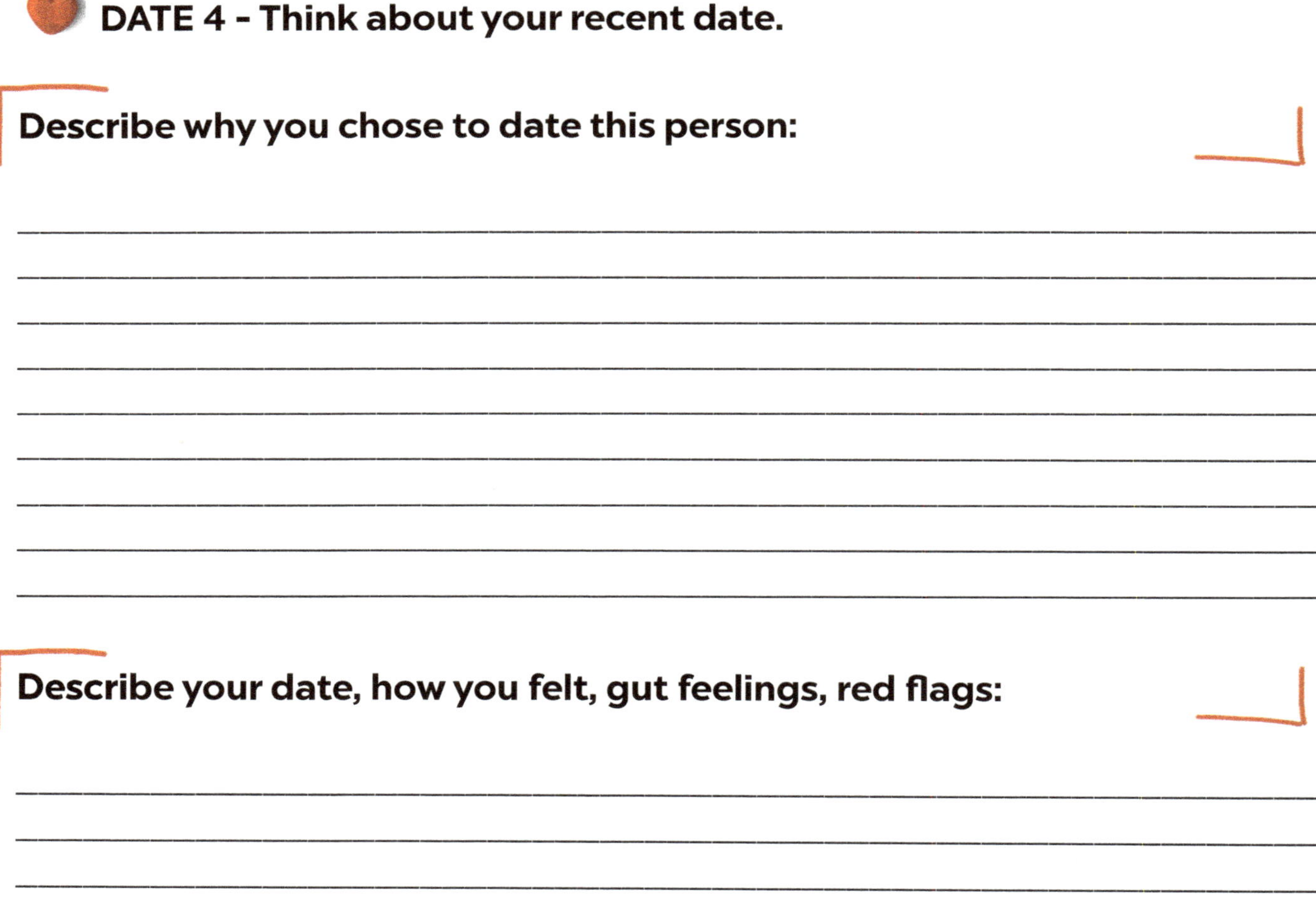

Describe why you chose to date this person:

Describe your date, how you felt, gut feelings, red flags:

Describe how you feel after your date about this person - both positives and any concerns:

How does this person align with my values, wants and needs, future plans and non-negotiables?

DATING WORKSHEET

DATE 5 - Think about your recent date.

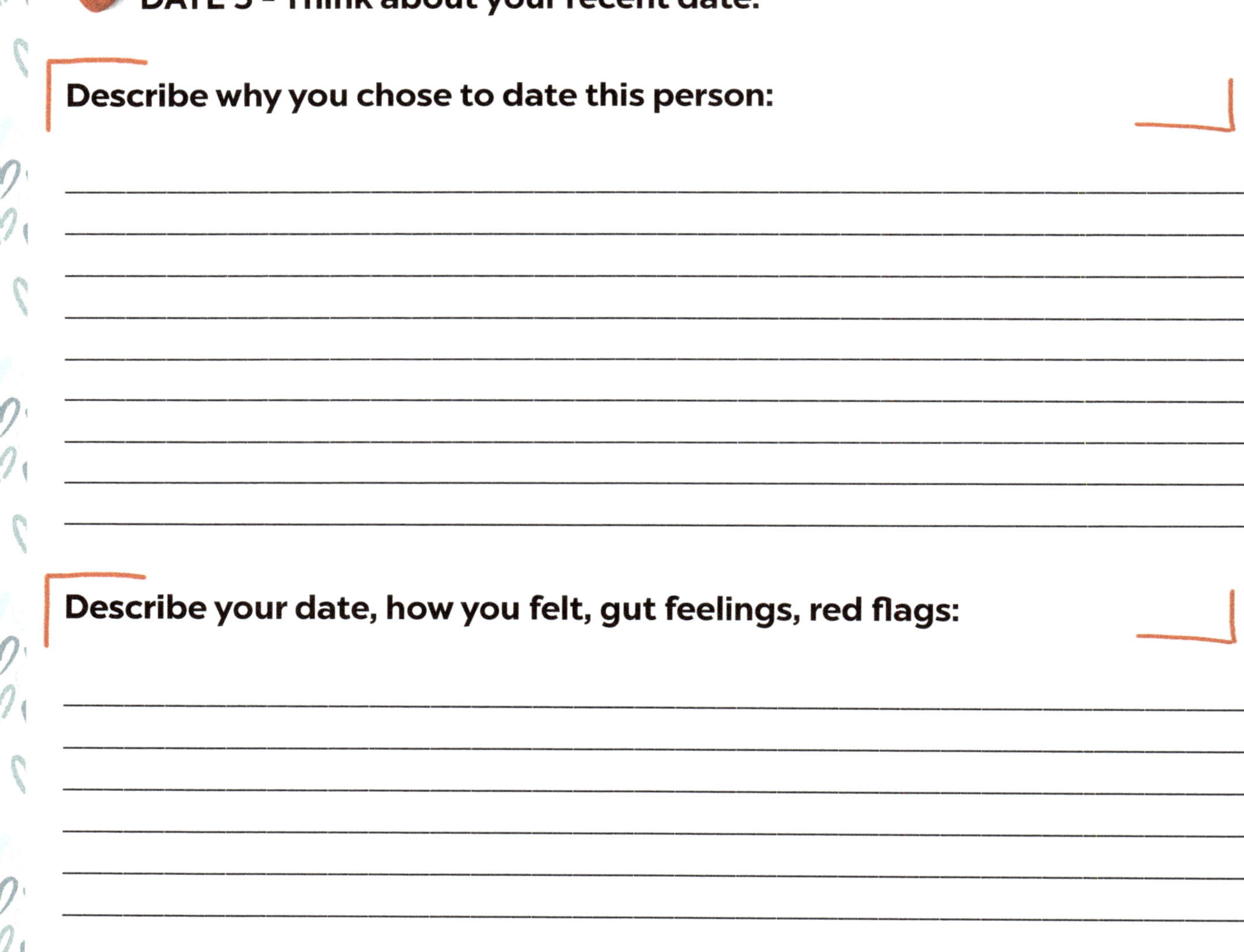

Describe why you chose to date this person:

Describe your date, how you felt, gut feelings, red flags:

Describe how you feel after your date about this person - both positives and any concerns:

How does this person align with my values, wants and needs, future plans and non-negotiables?

www.ingramcontent.com/pod-product-compliance
Ingram Content Group UK Ltd.
Pitfield, Milton Keynes, MK11 3LW, UK
UKHW061951290726
14090UKWH00021B/1173

9 780645 527469